MORE BOOK, FREEBIE PAGES : K-IMAGINE-PUB.COM

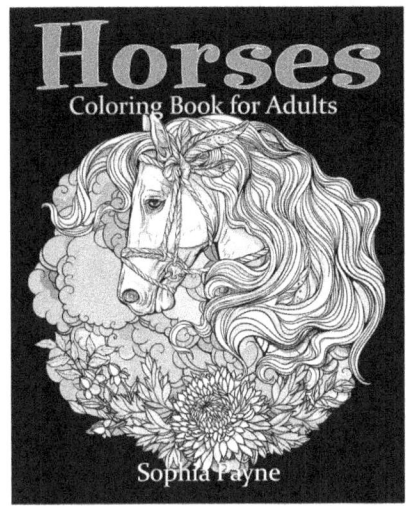
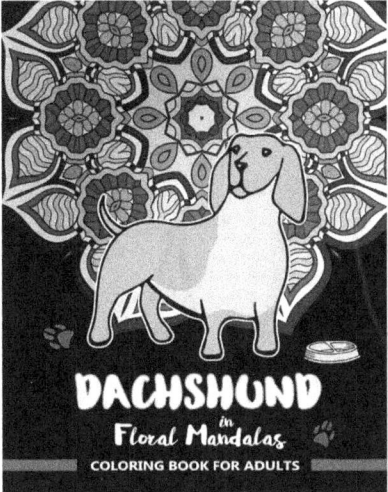

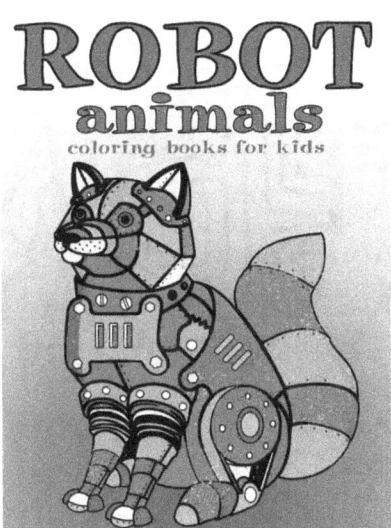
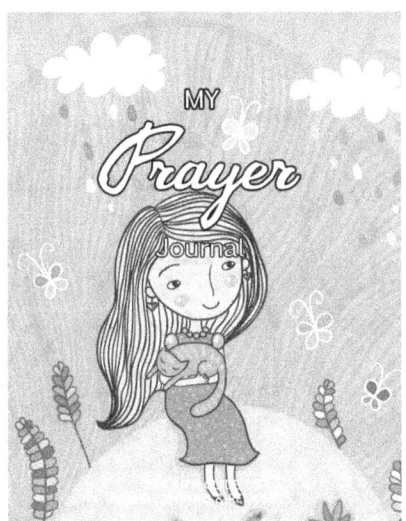
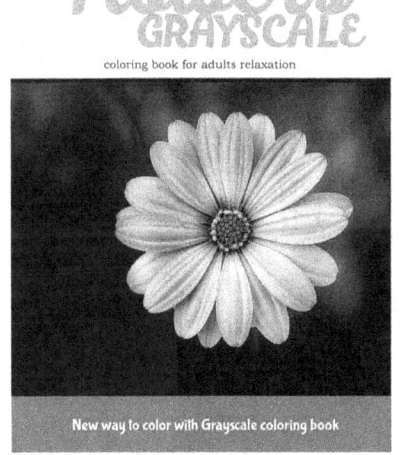
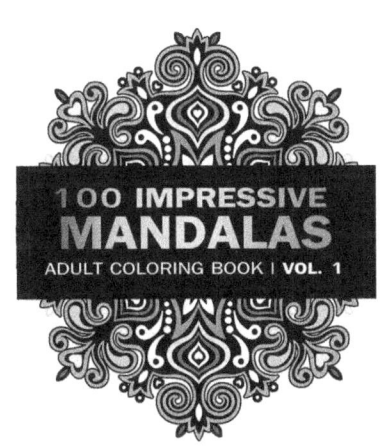
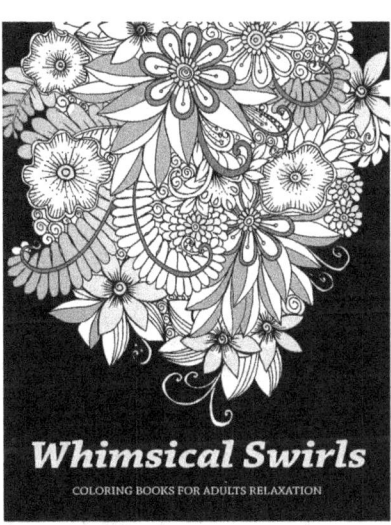
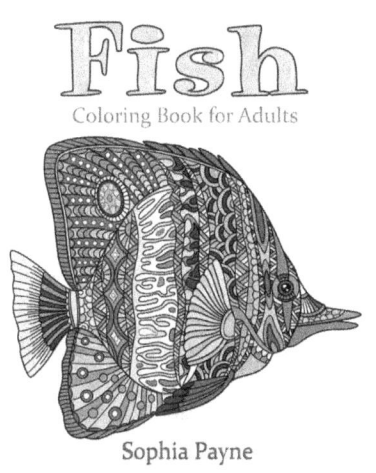

Copyright: Published in the United States

Copyright: Published in the United States

All rights reserved.

- Color Test Page -

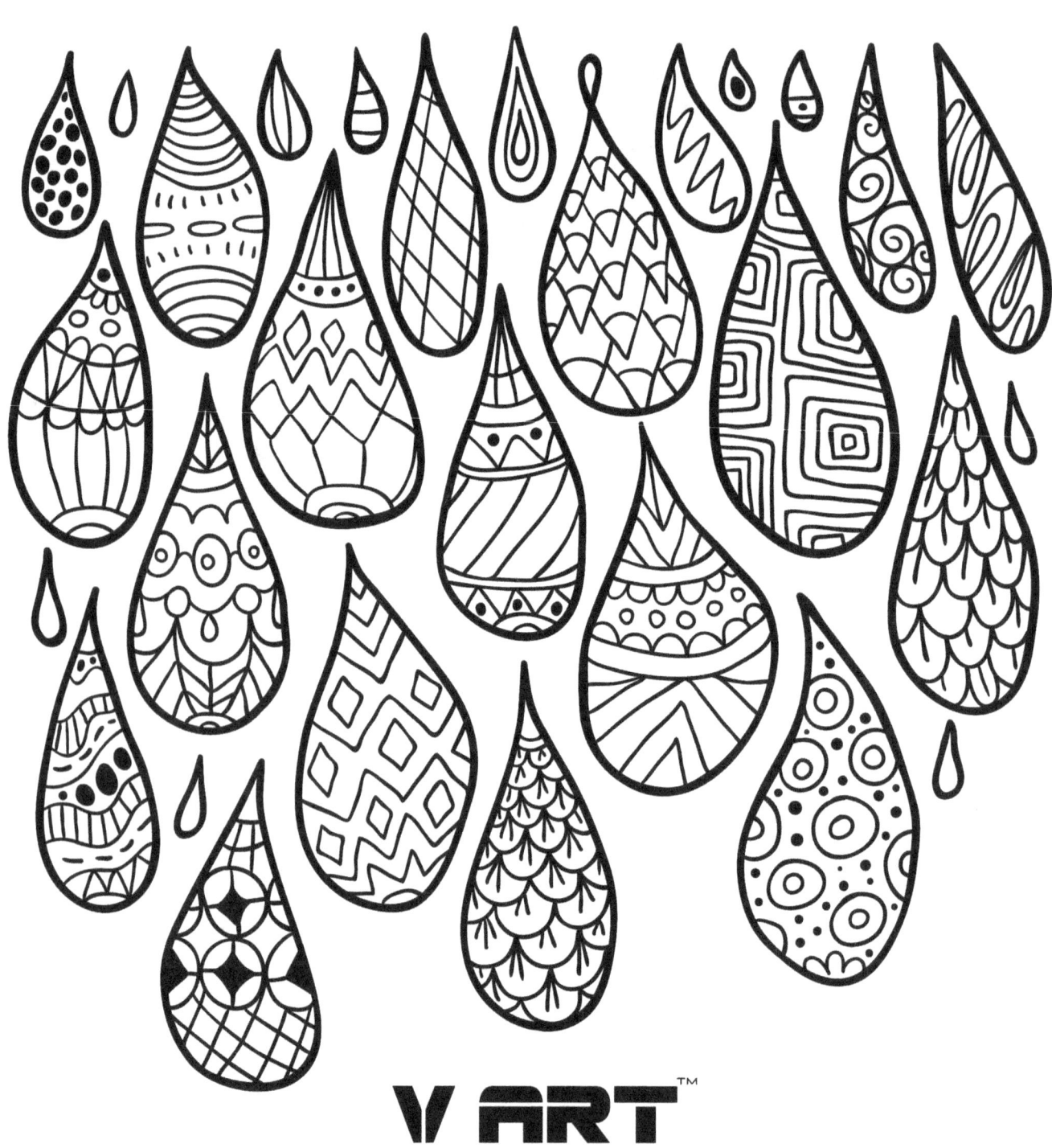

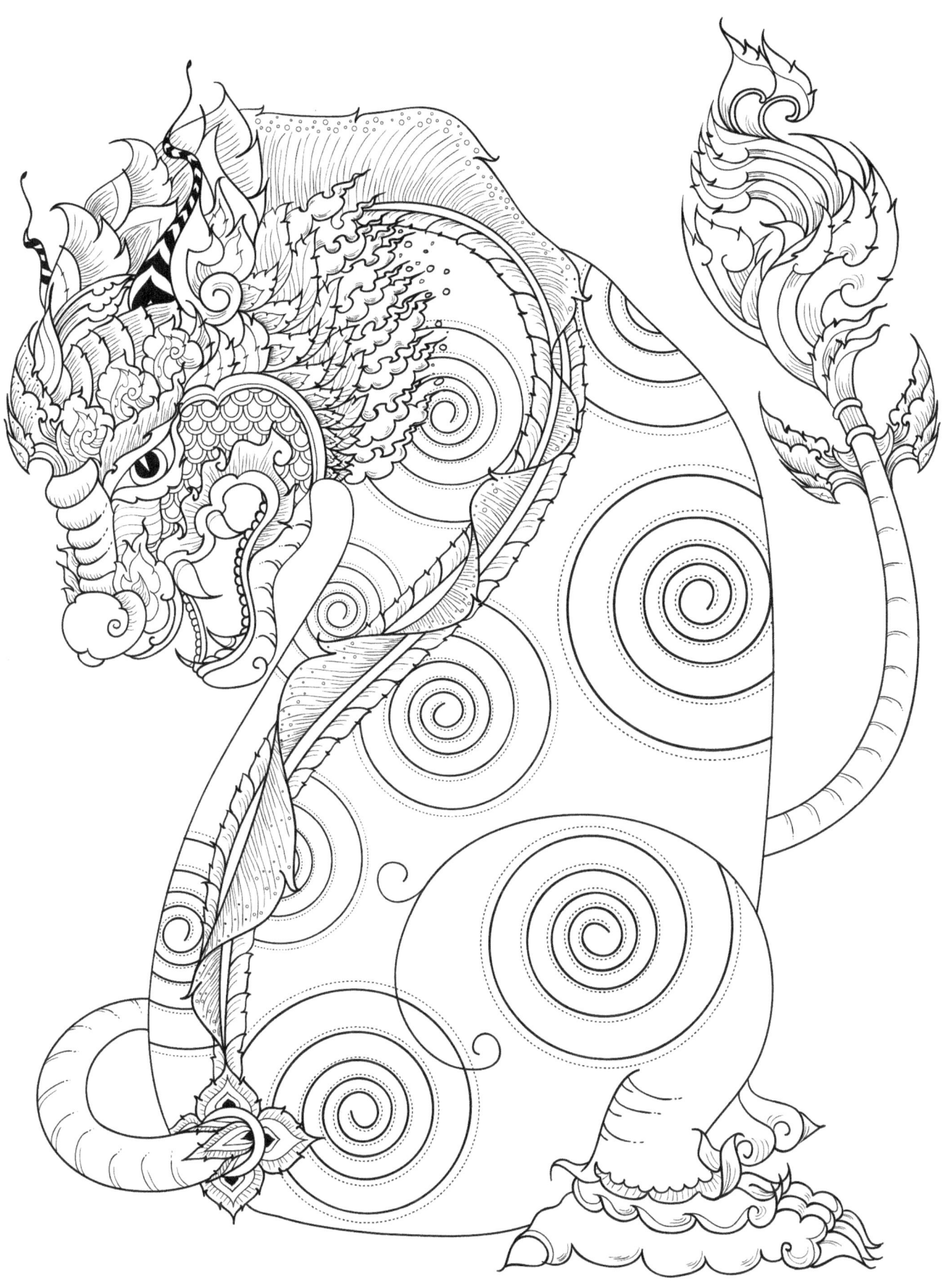

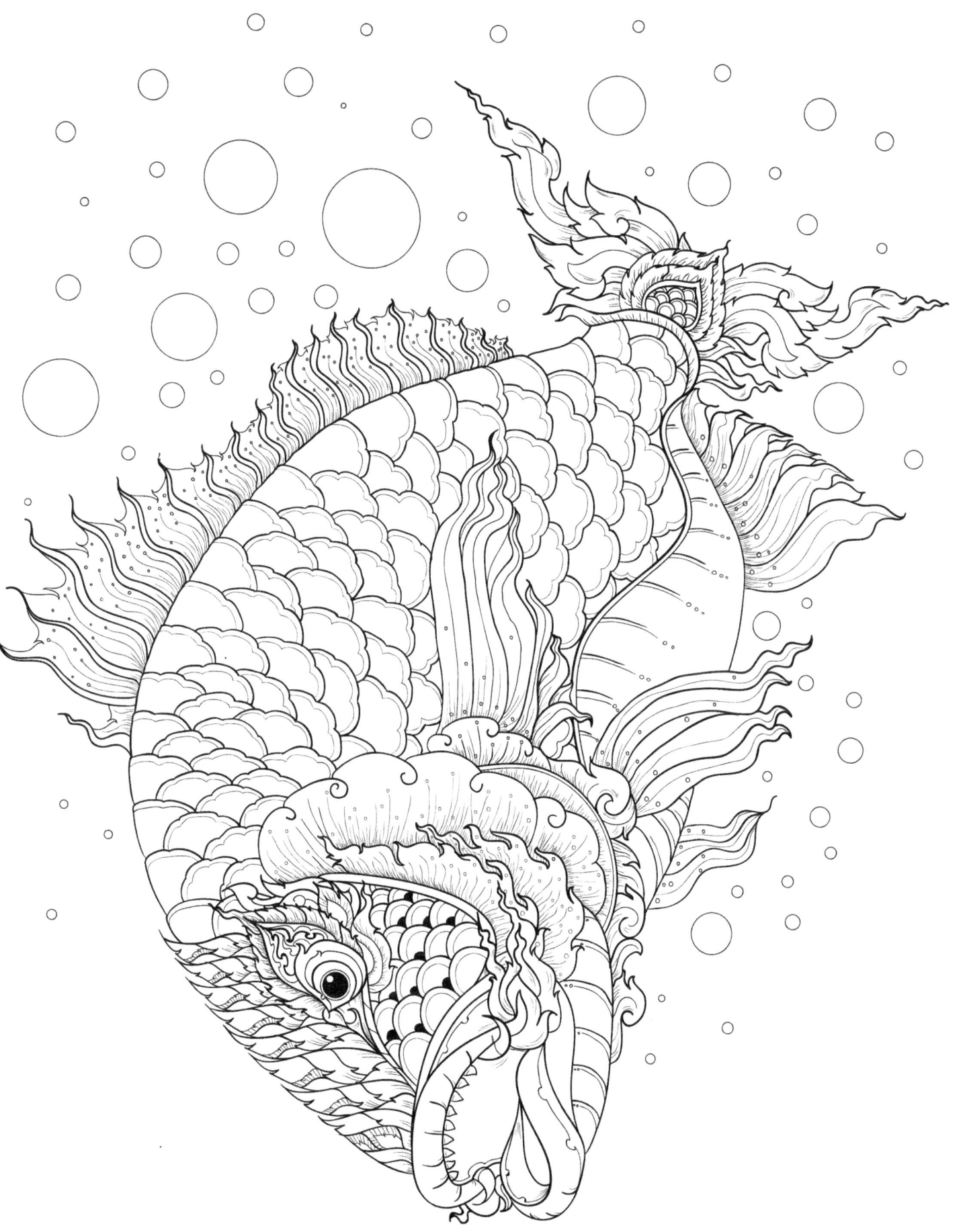

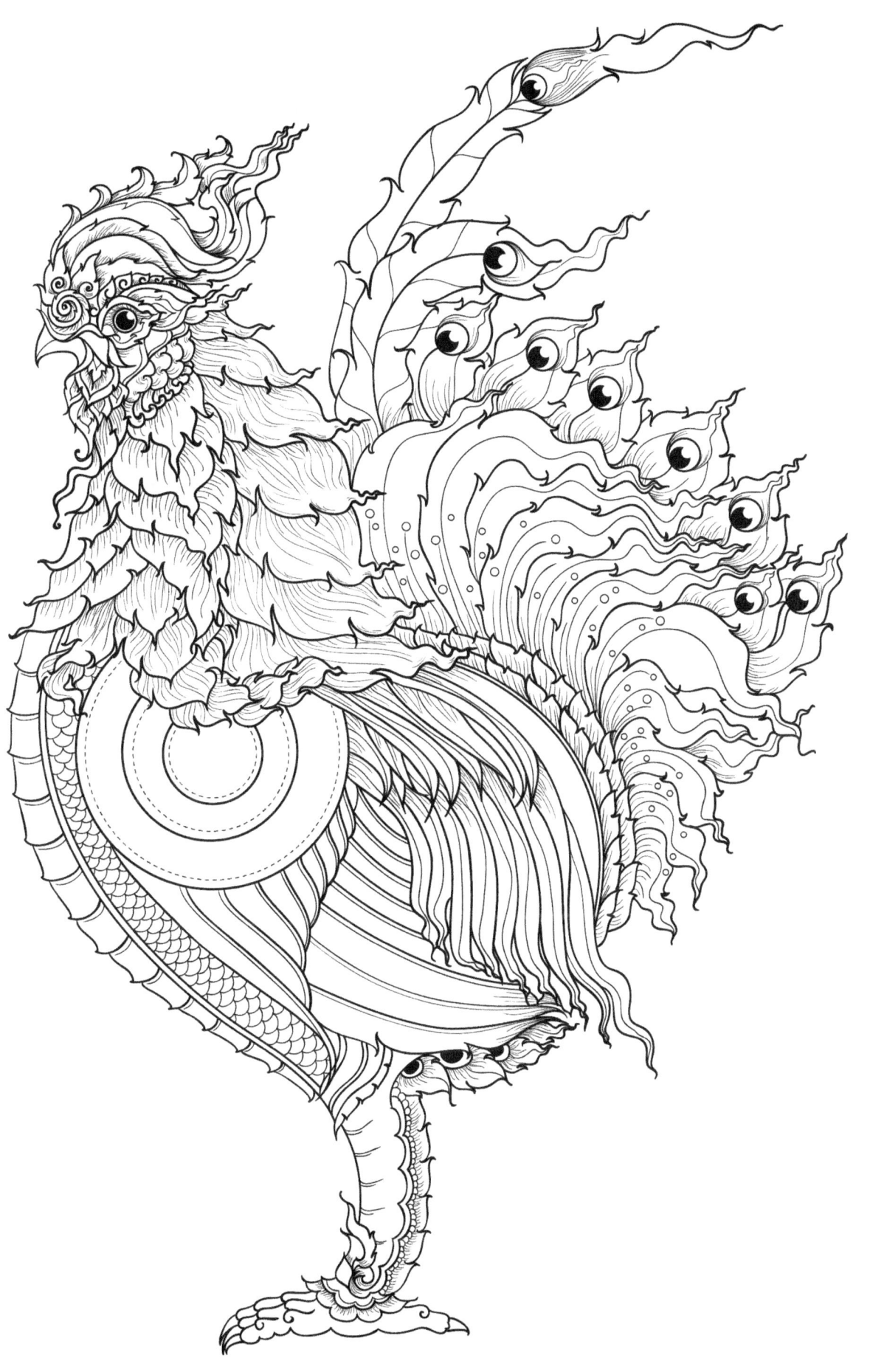

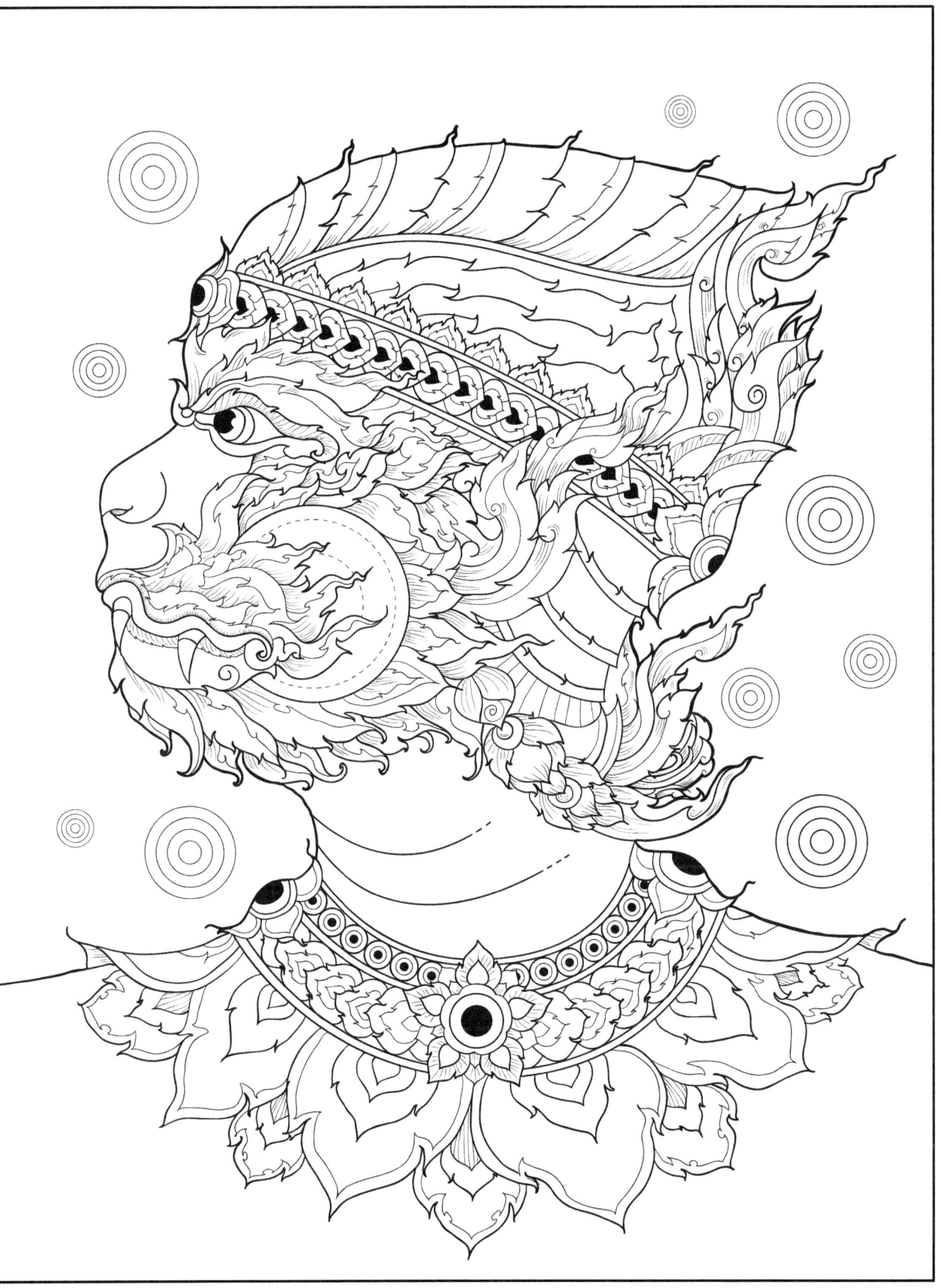

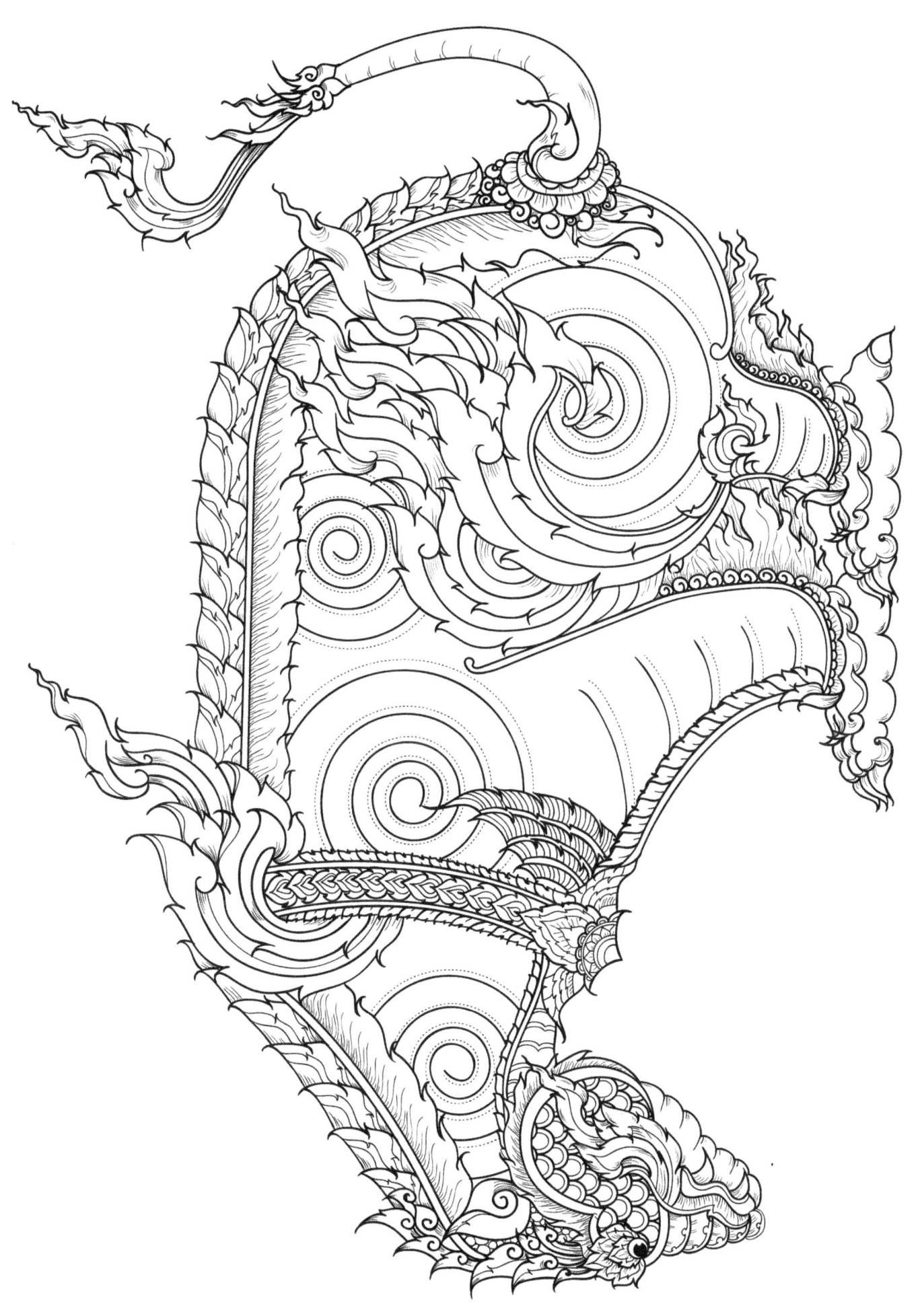

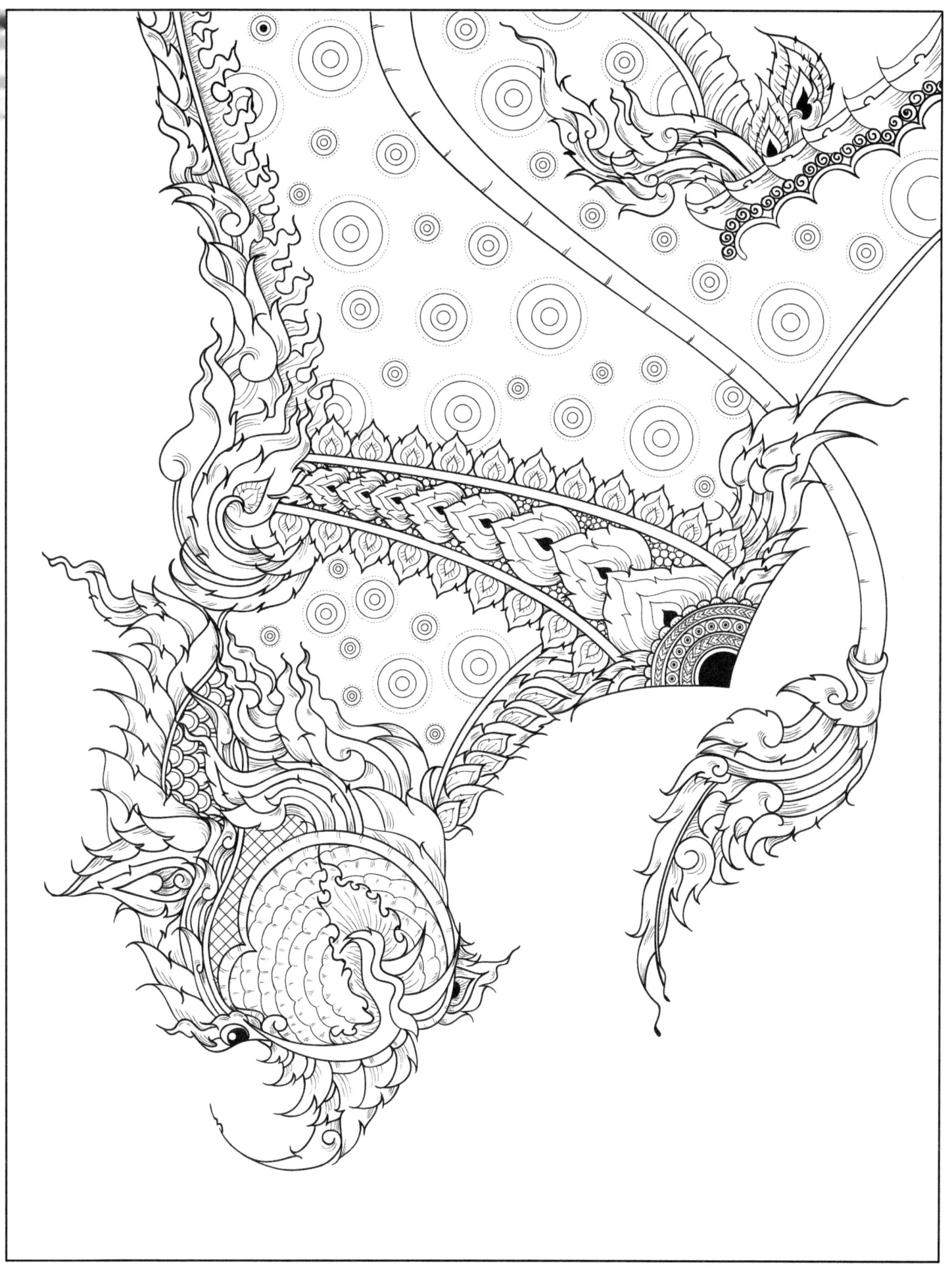

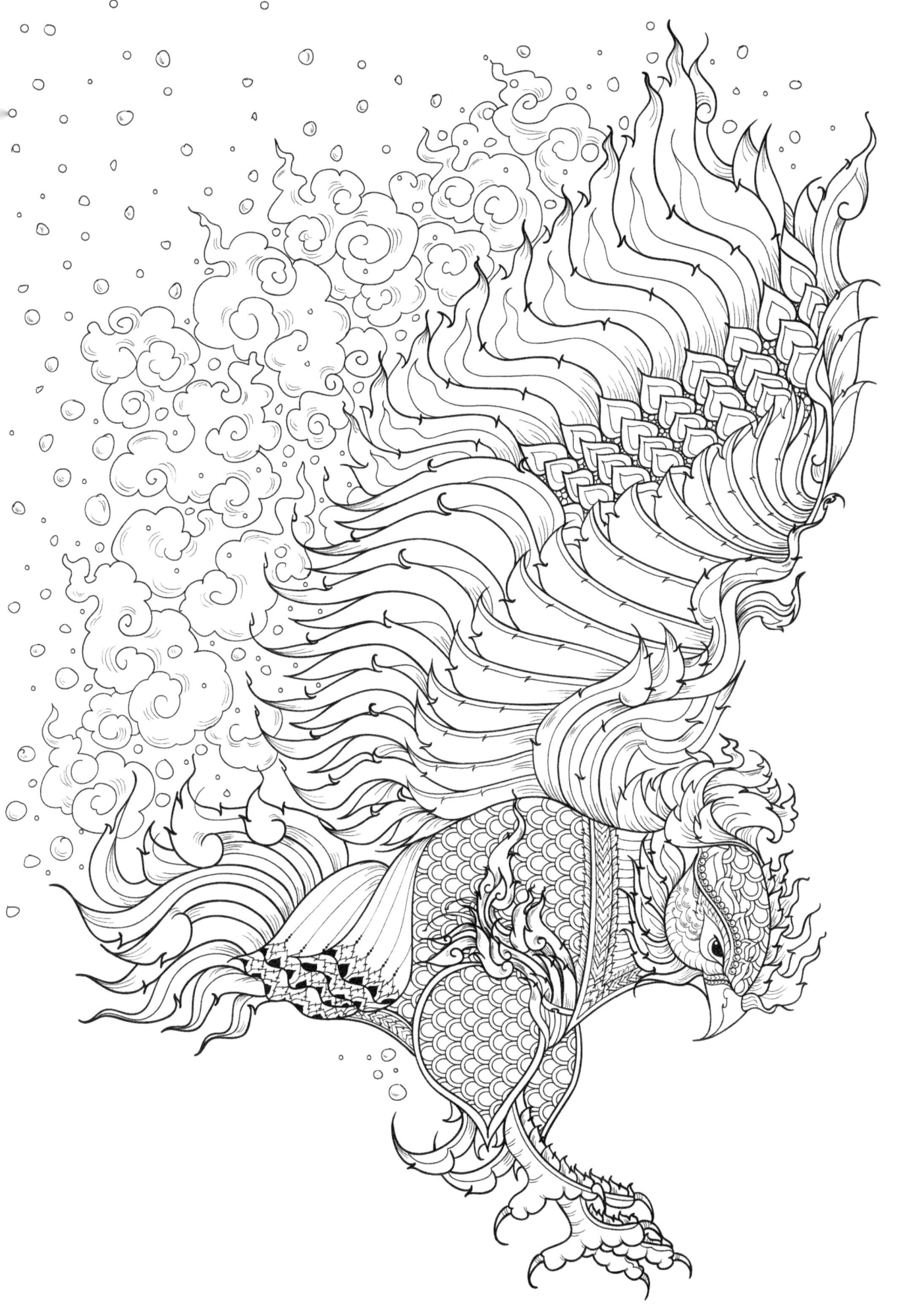

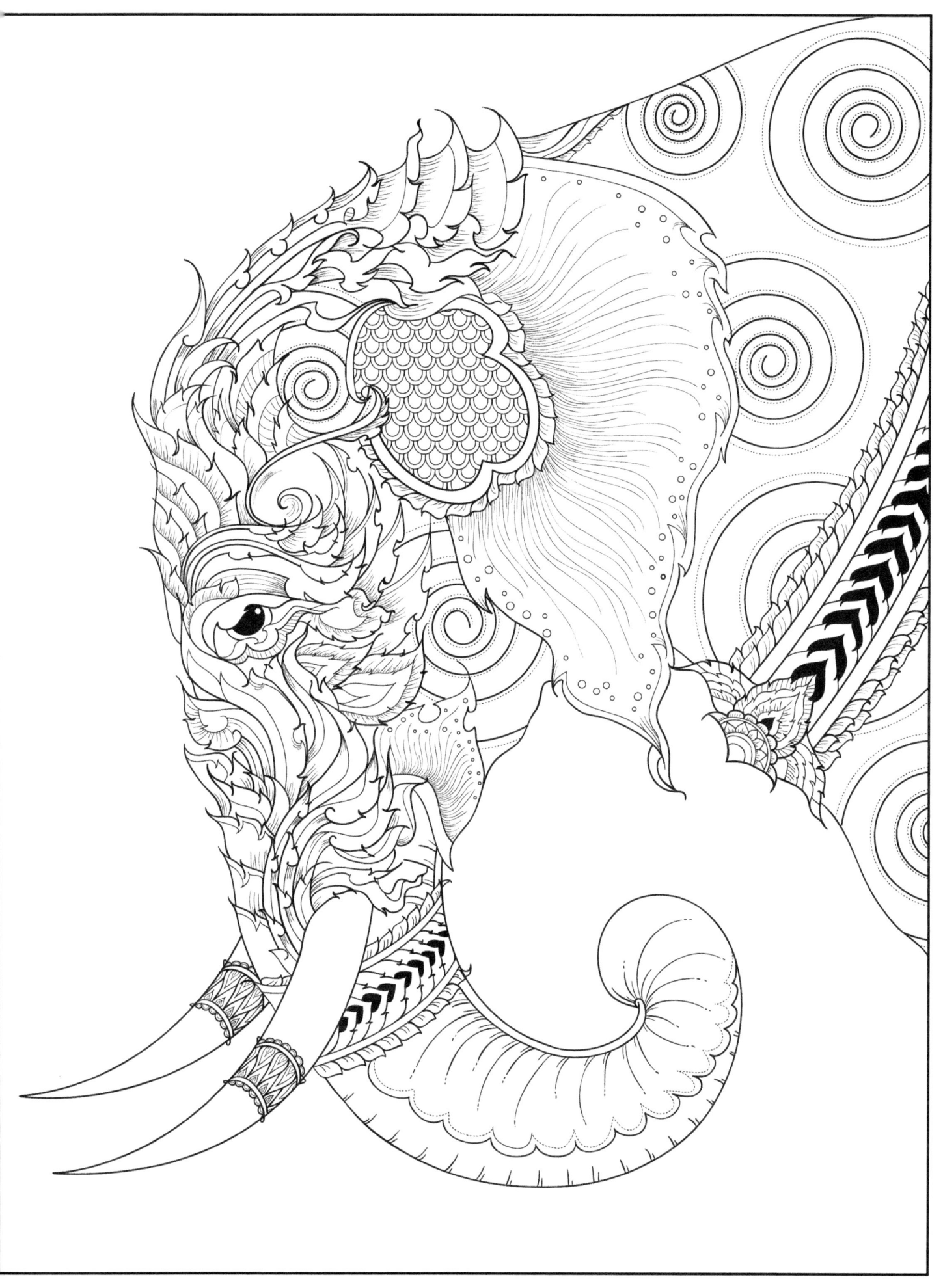

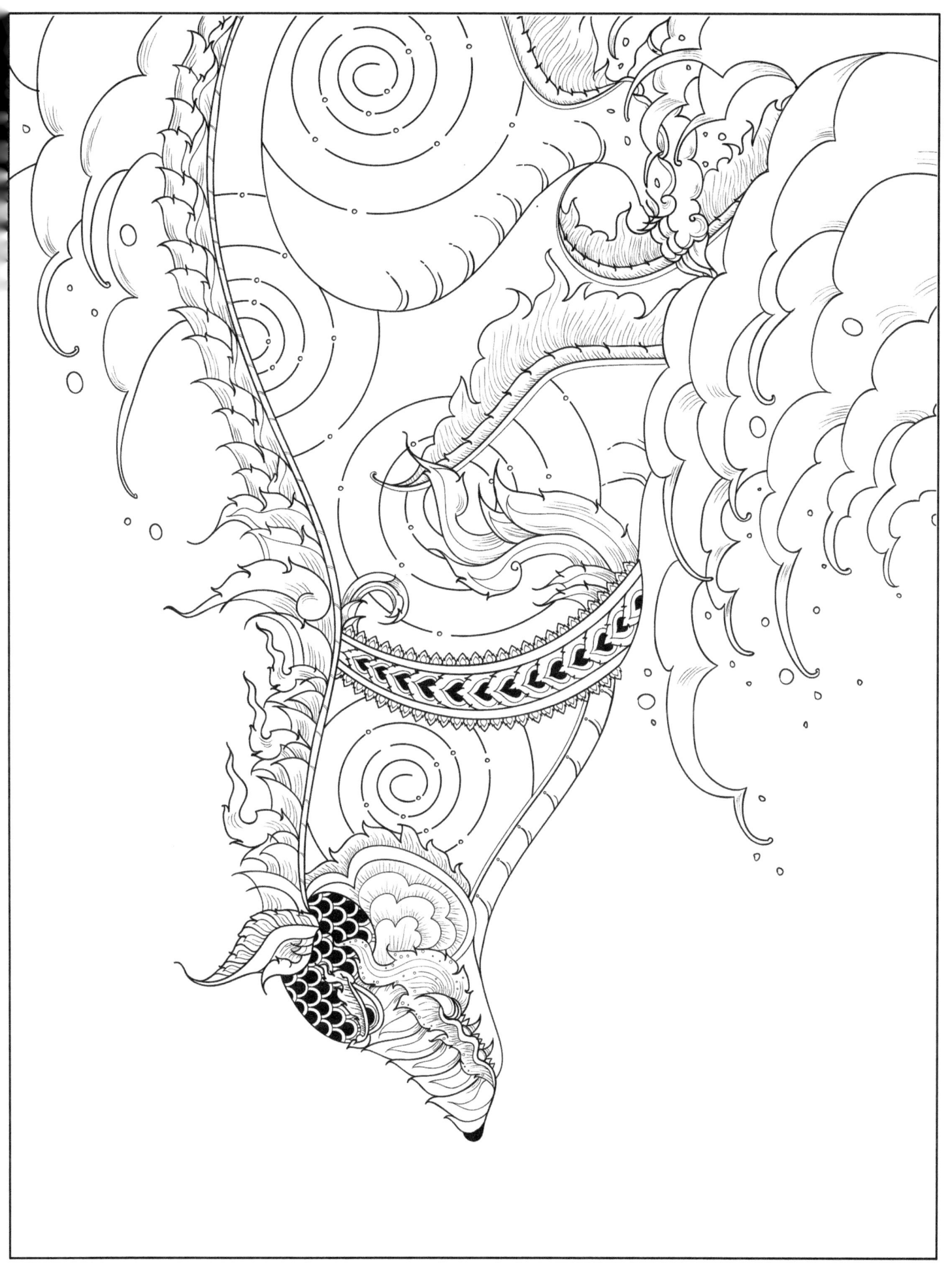

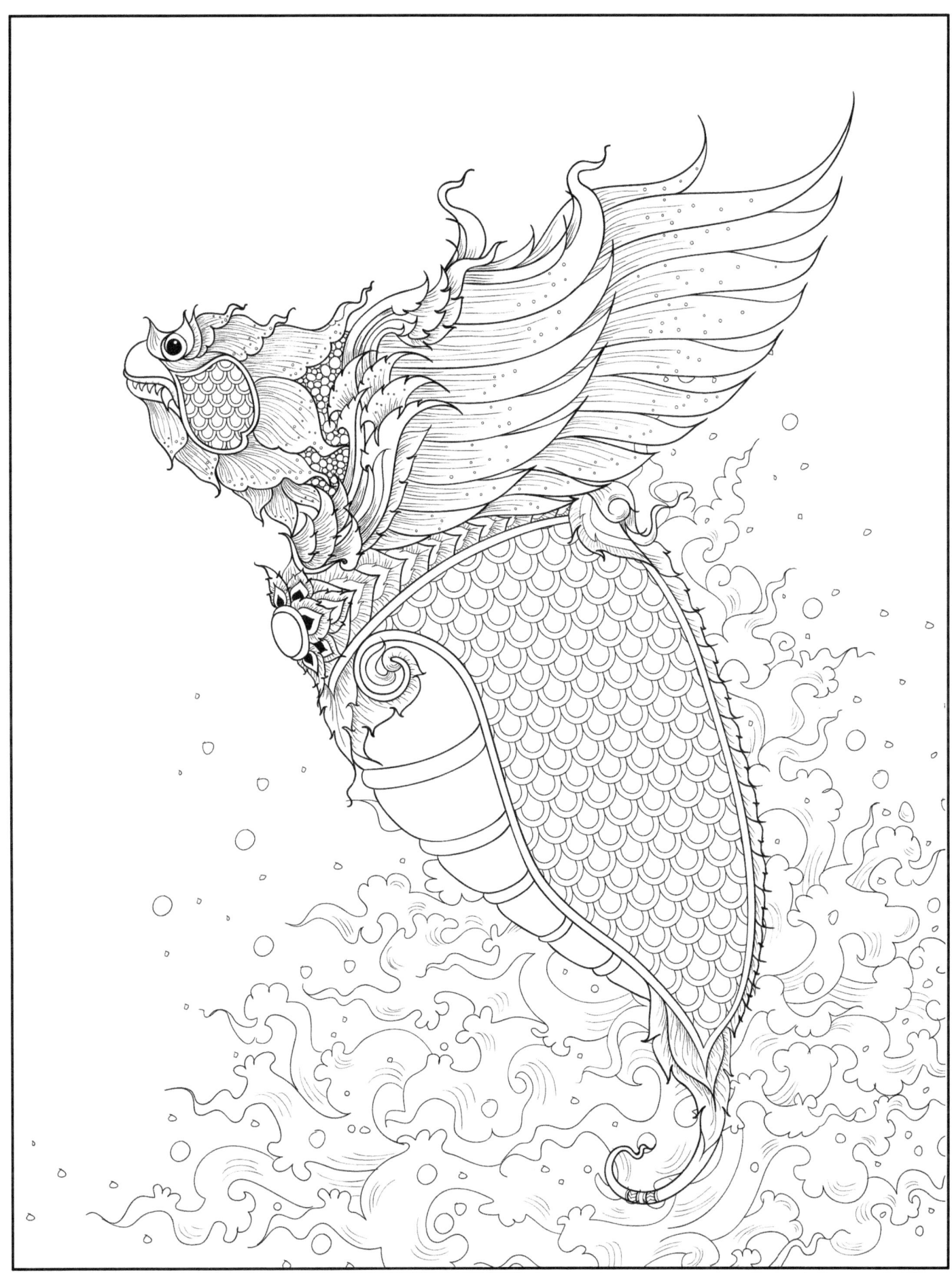

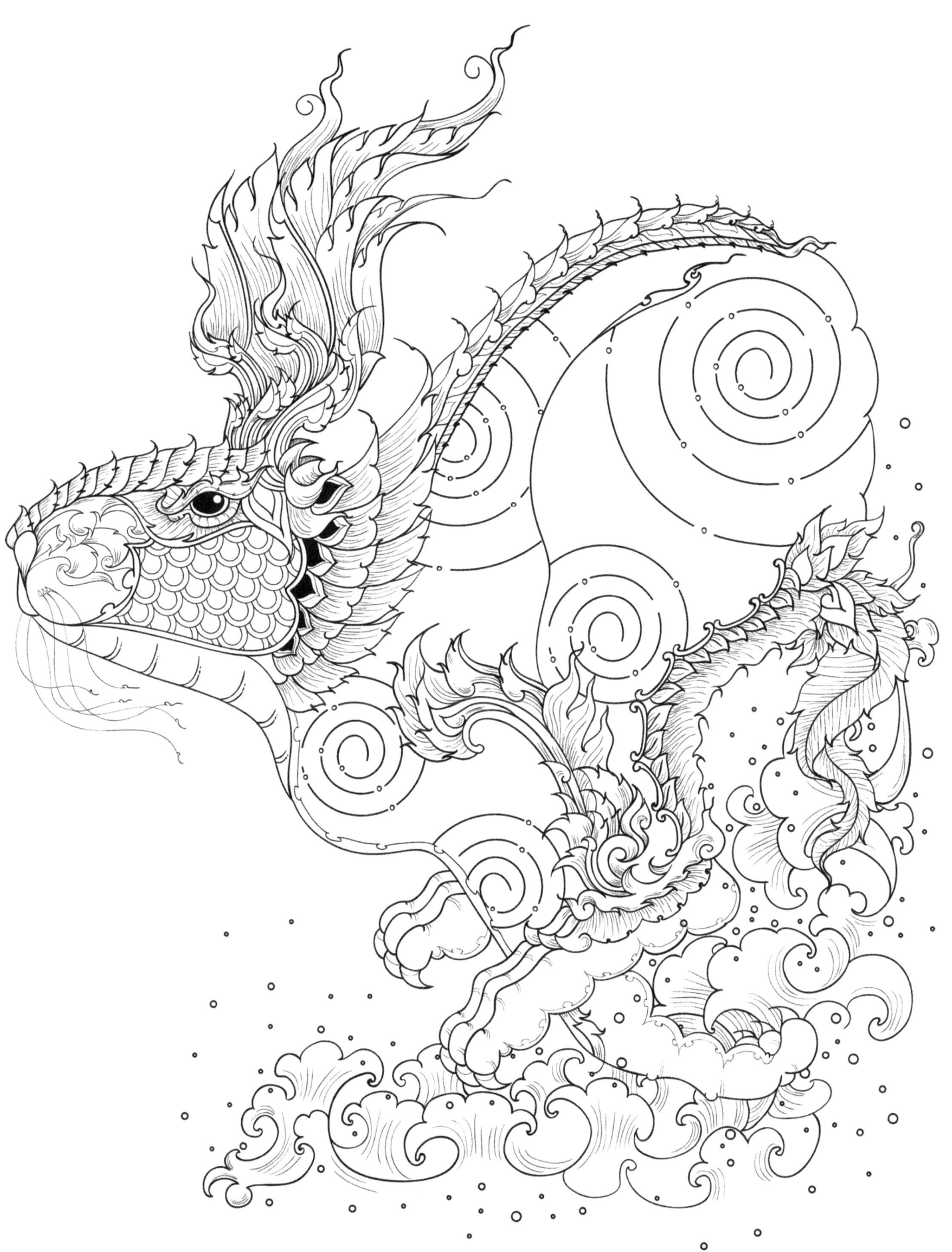

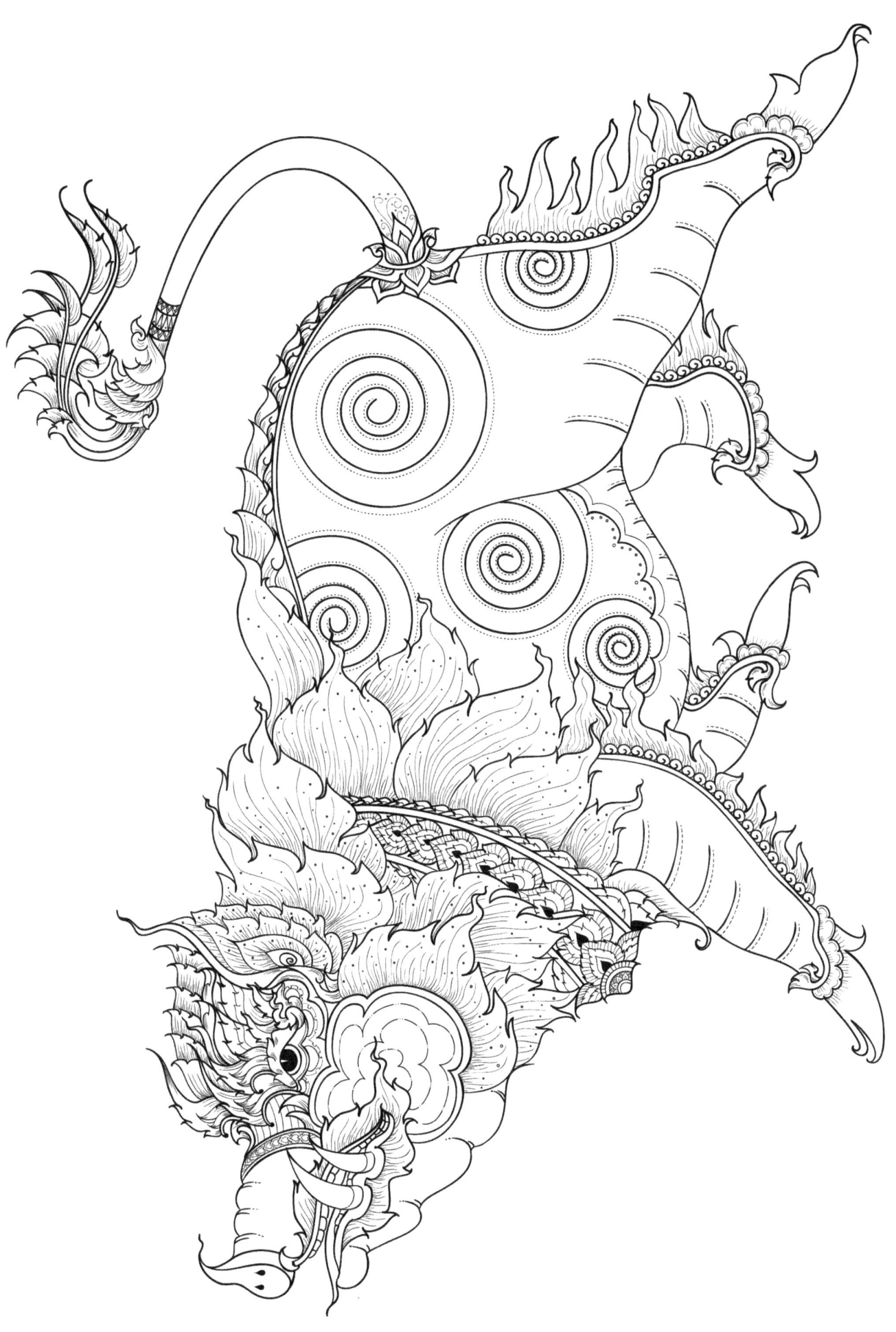

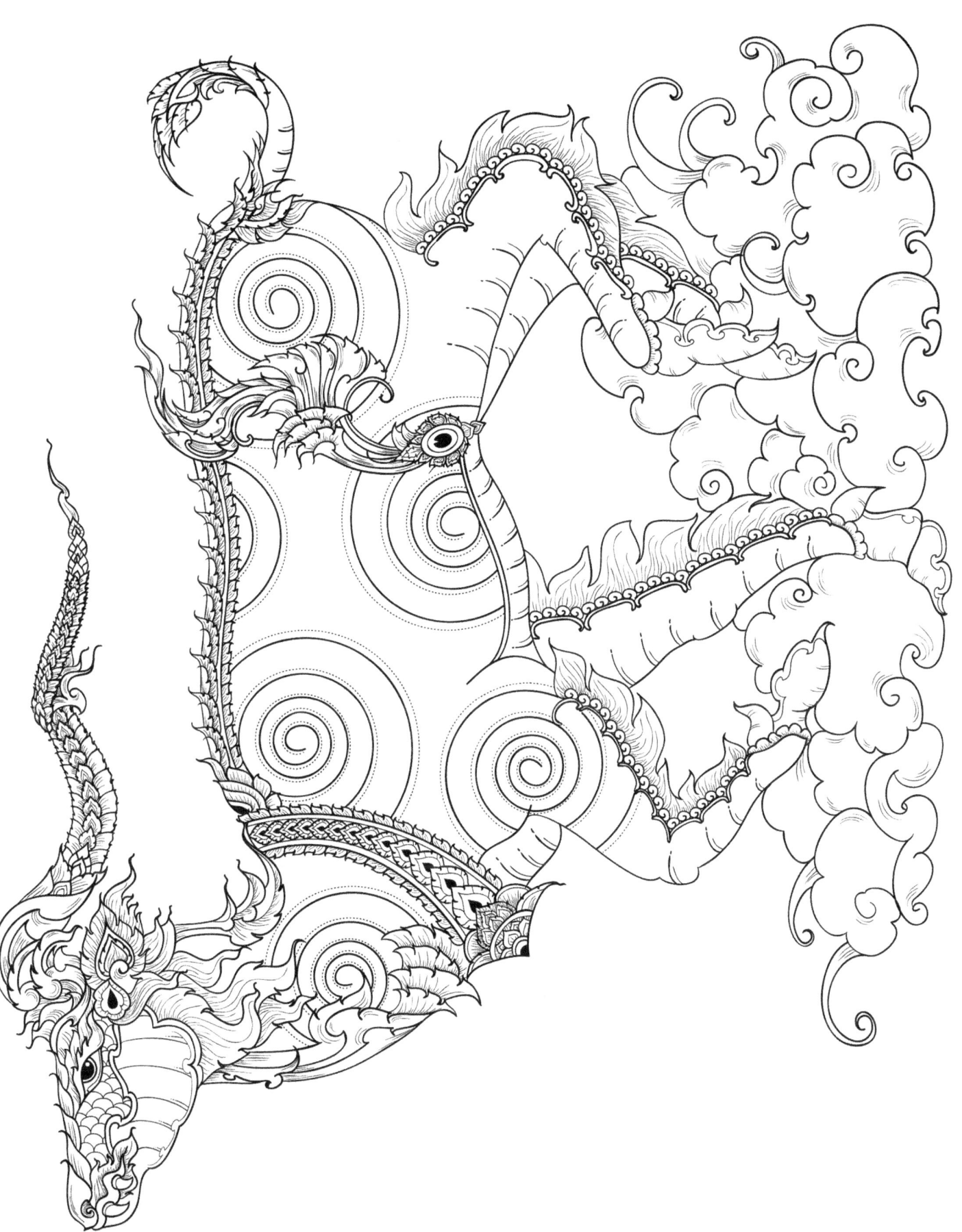

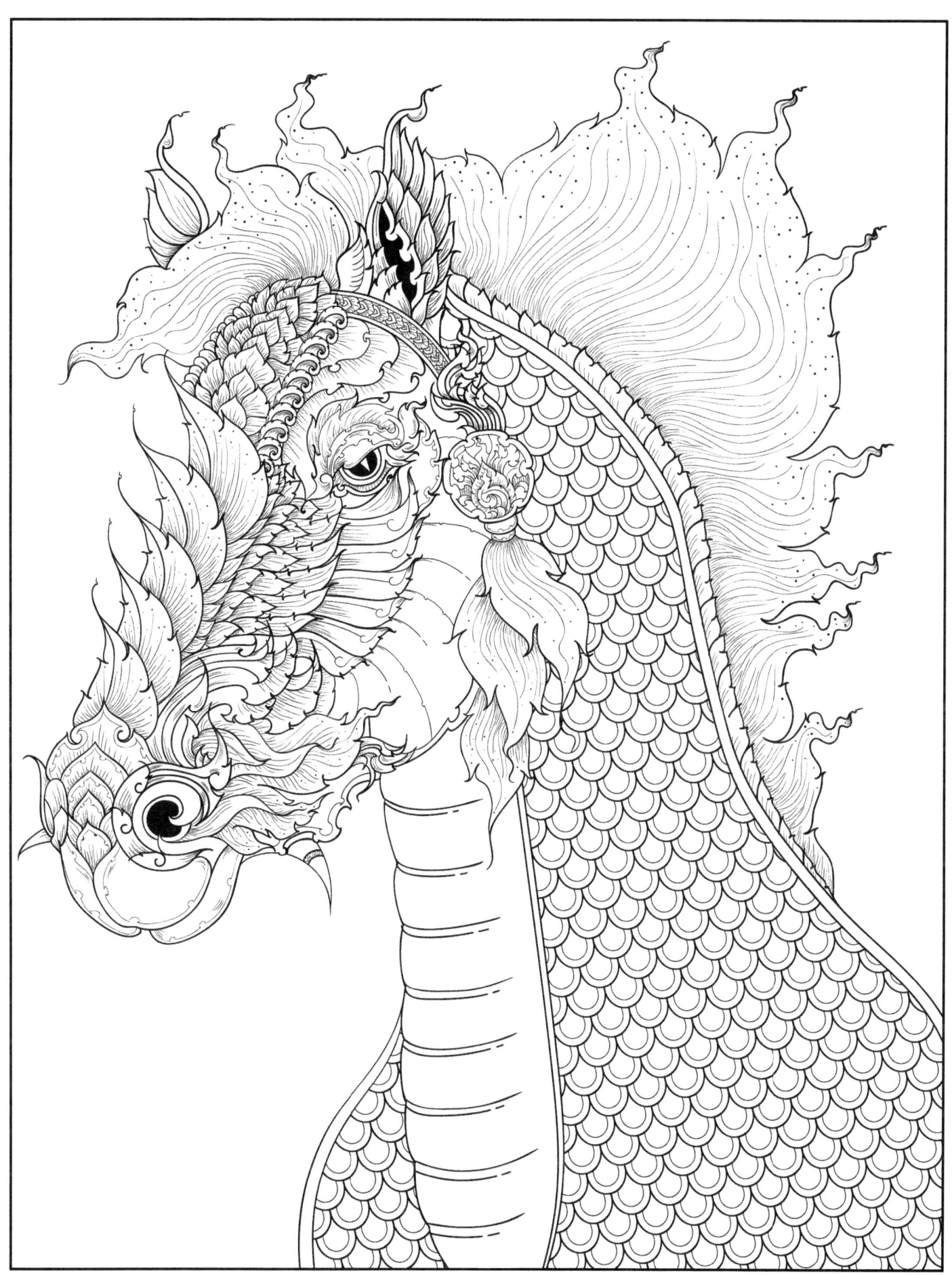

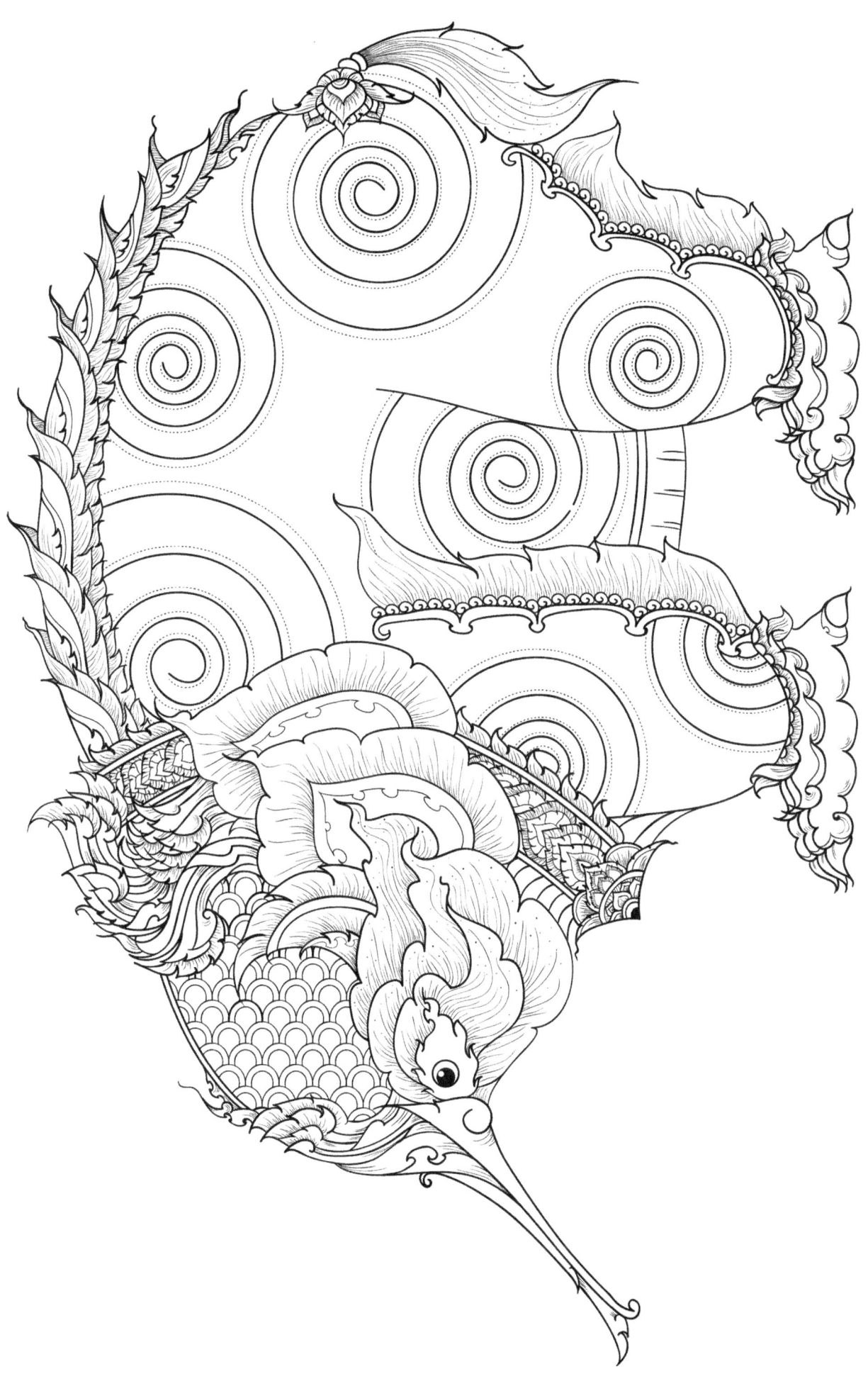

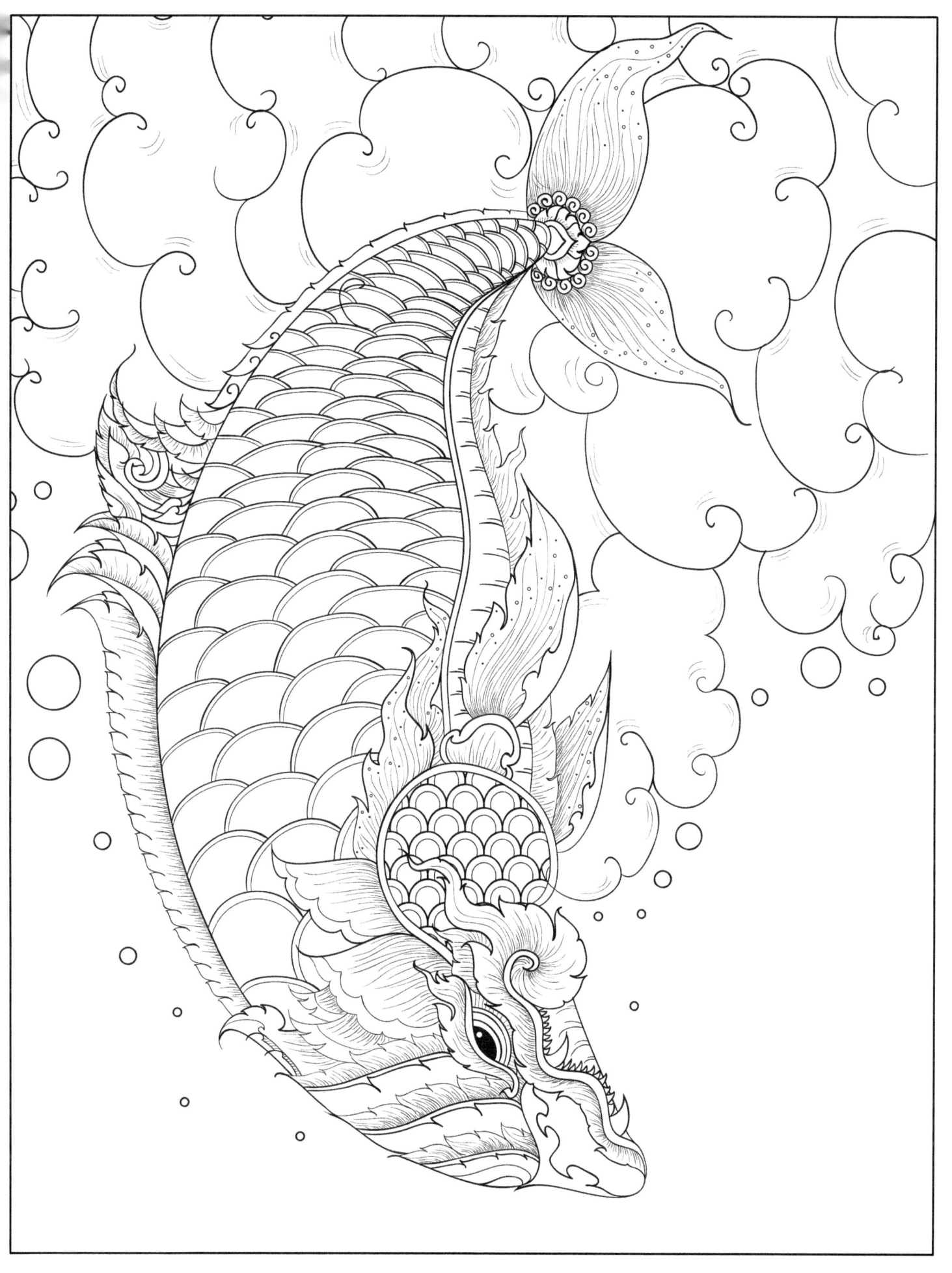

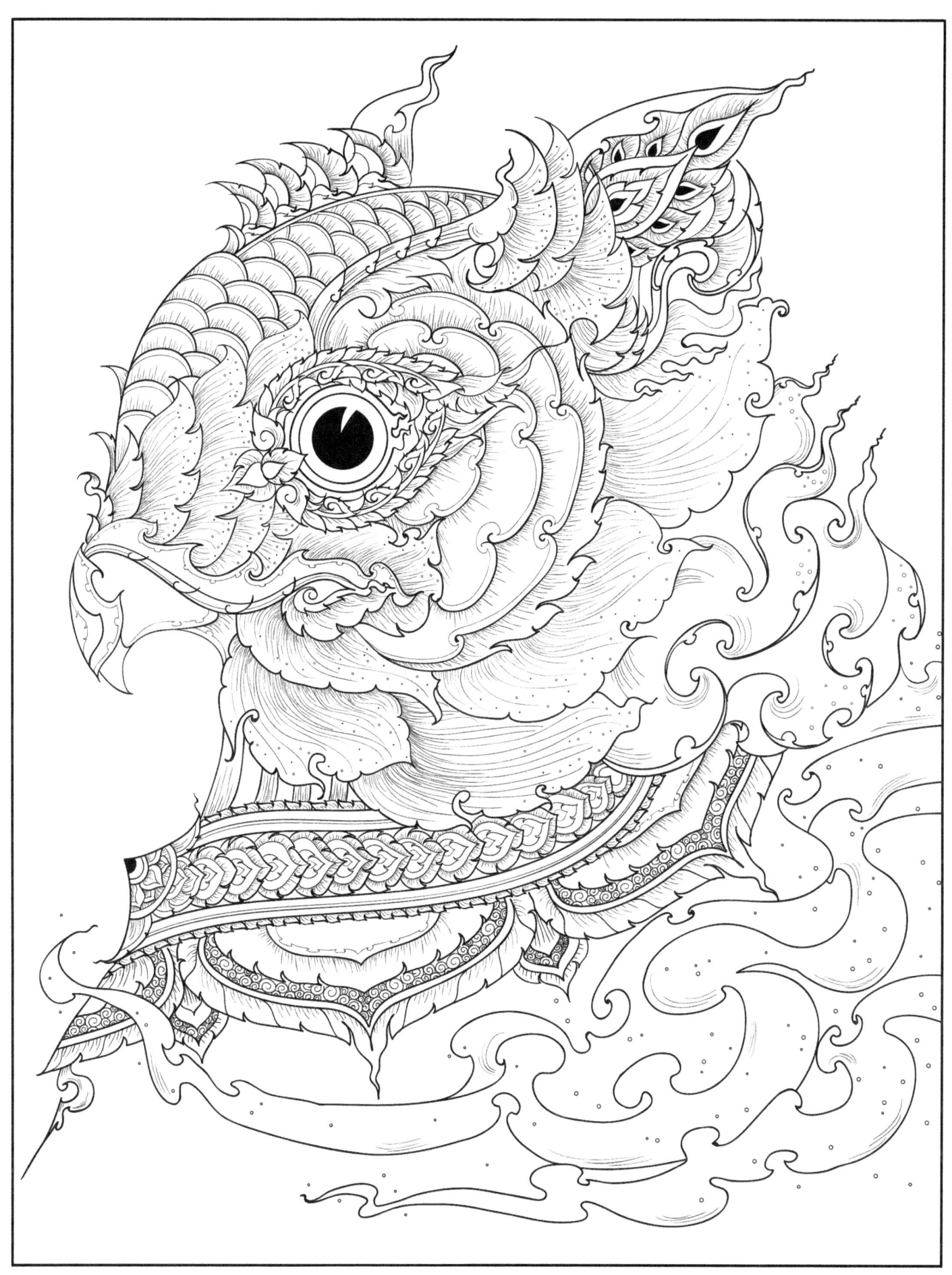

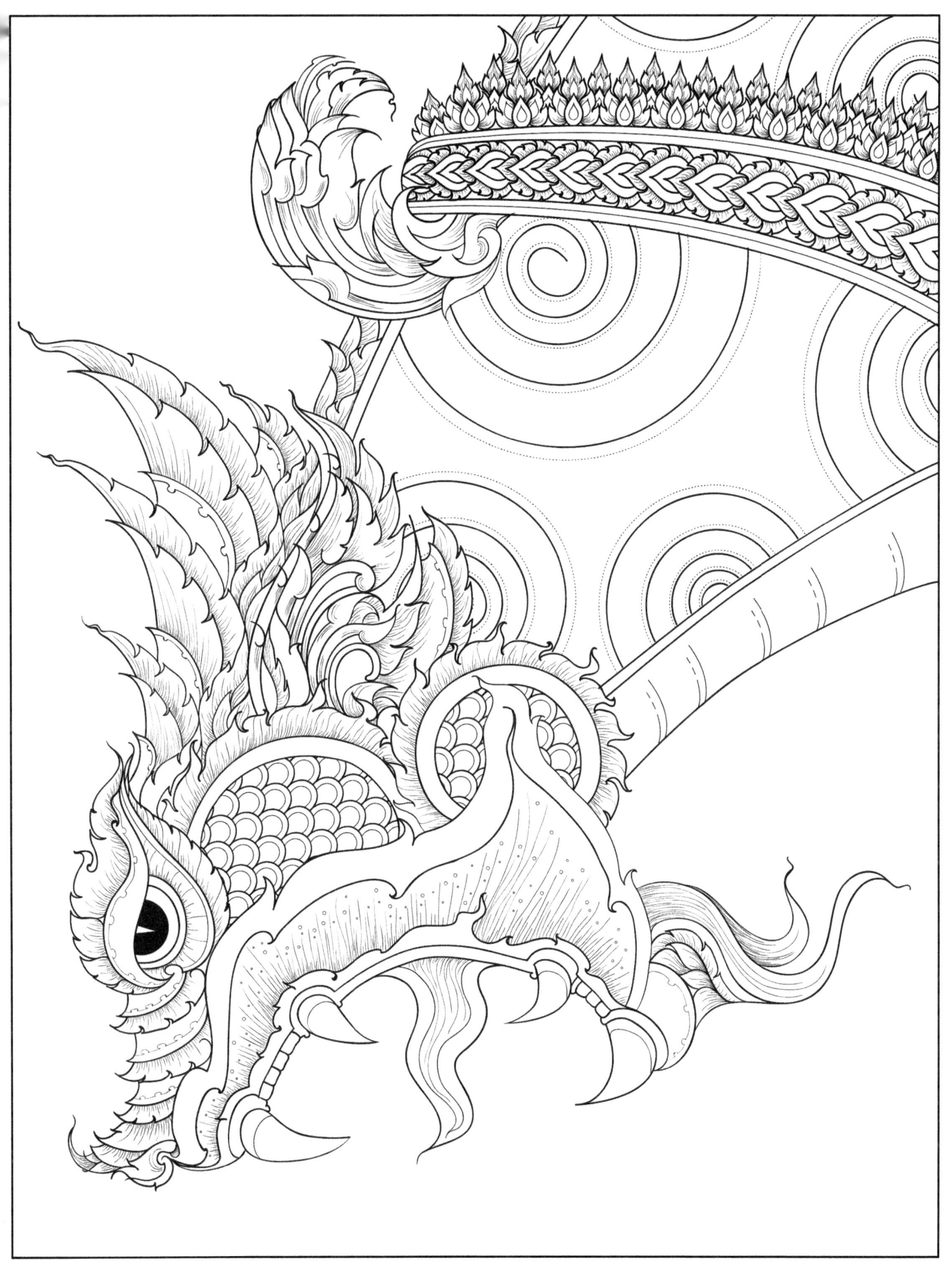

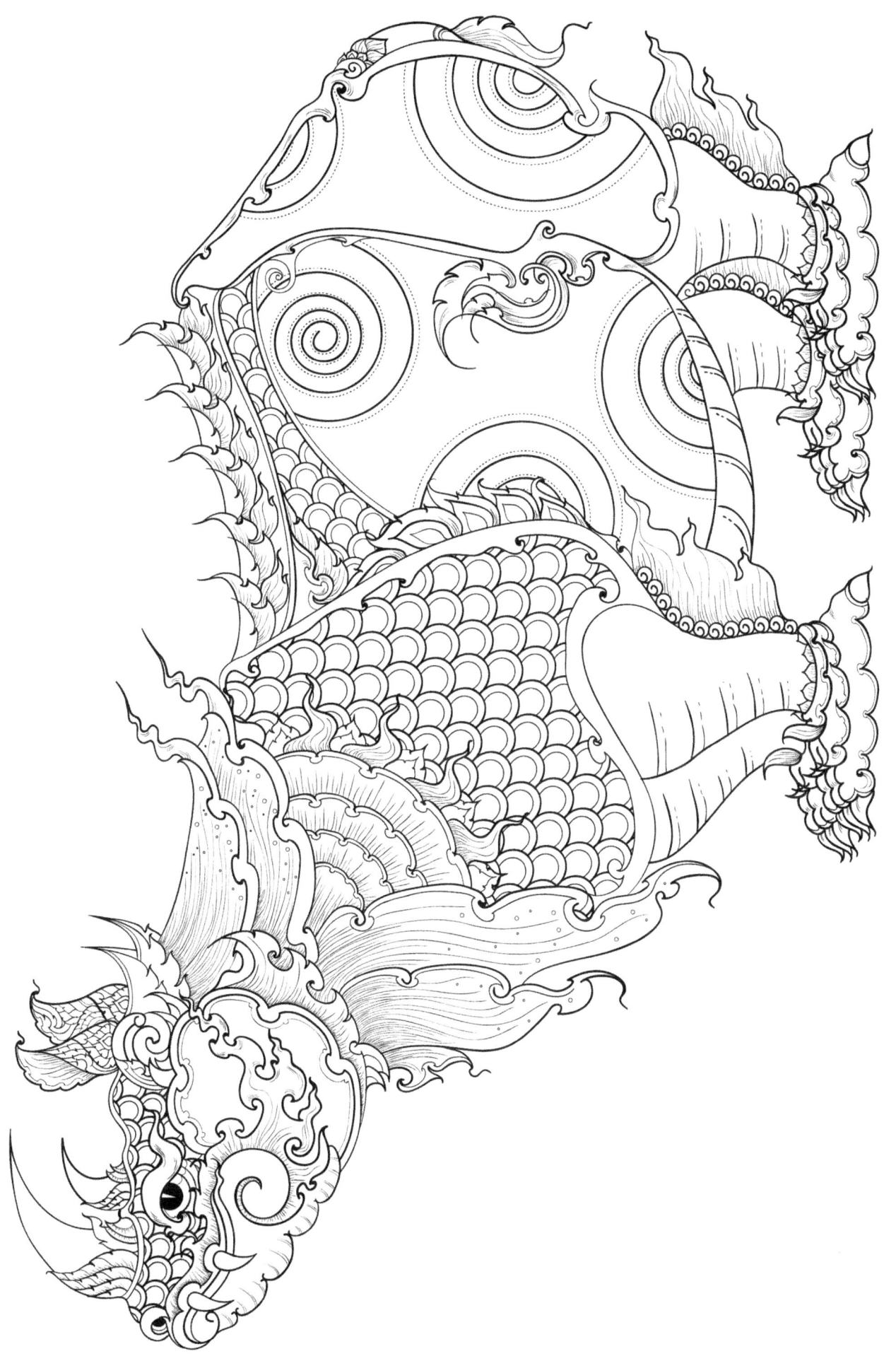

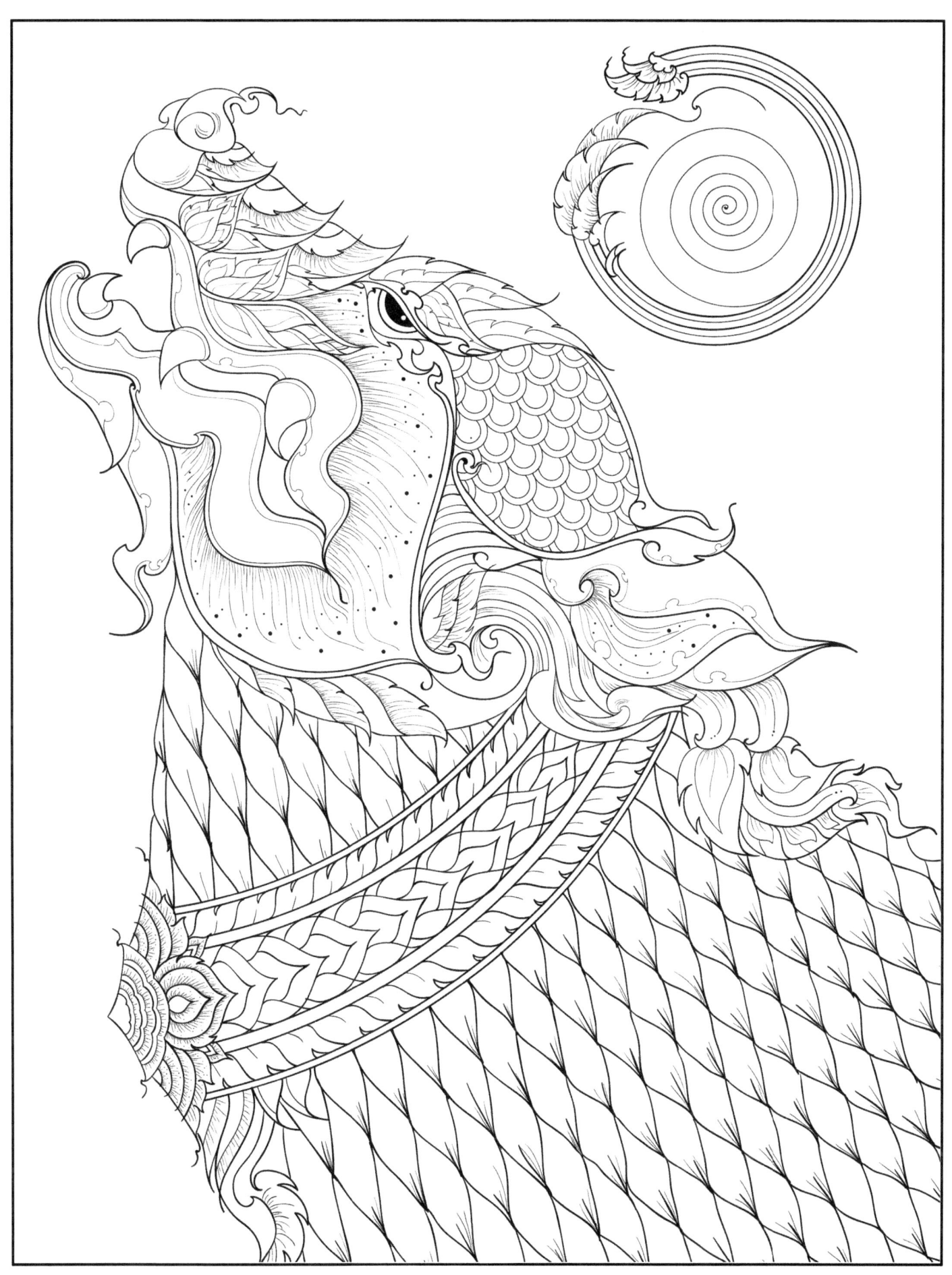

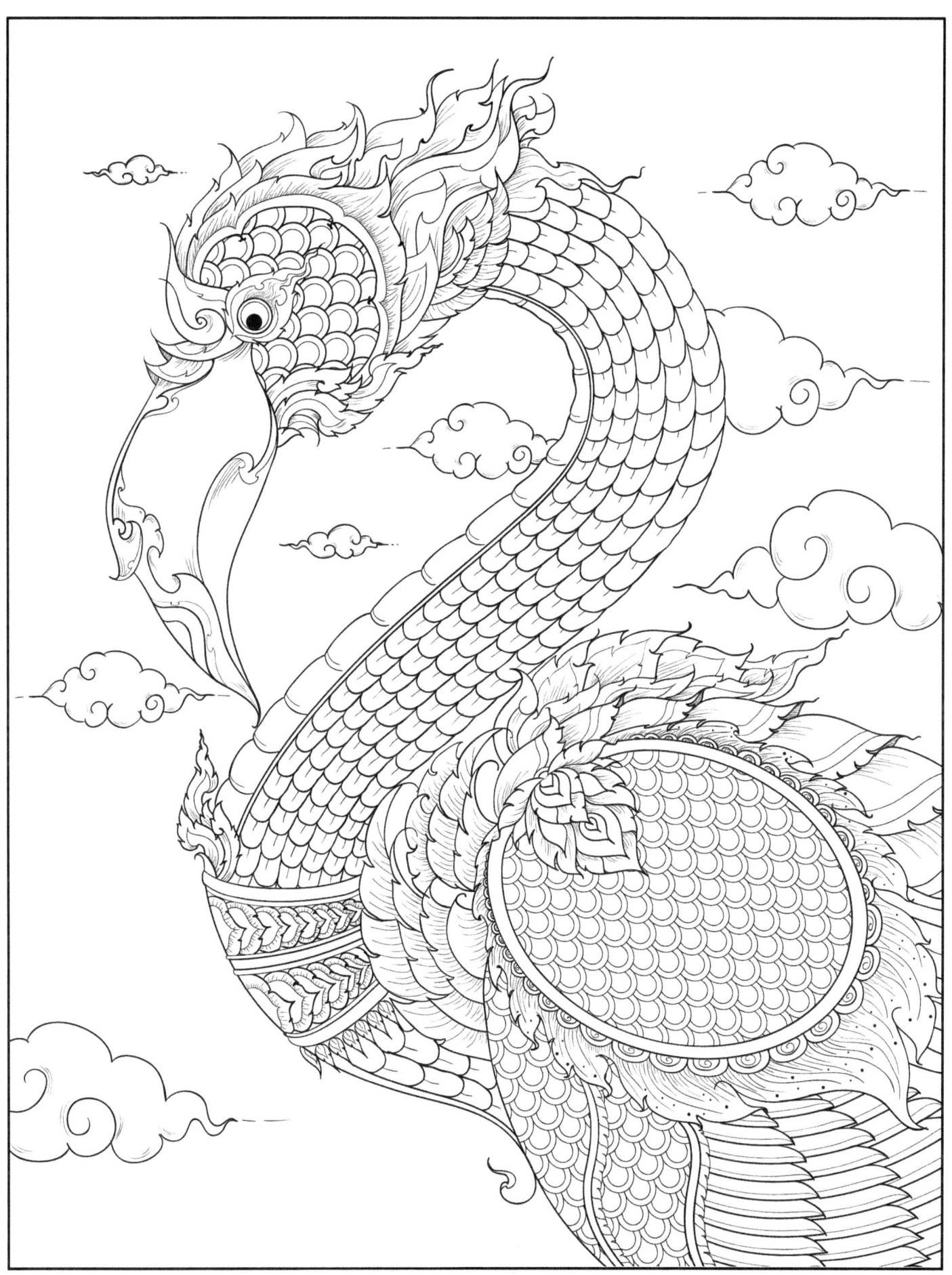

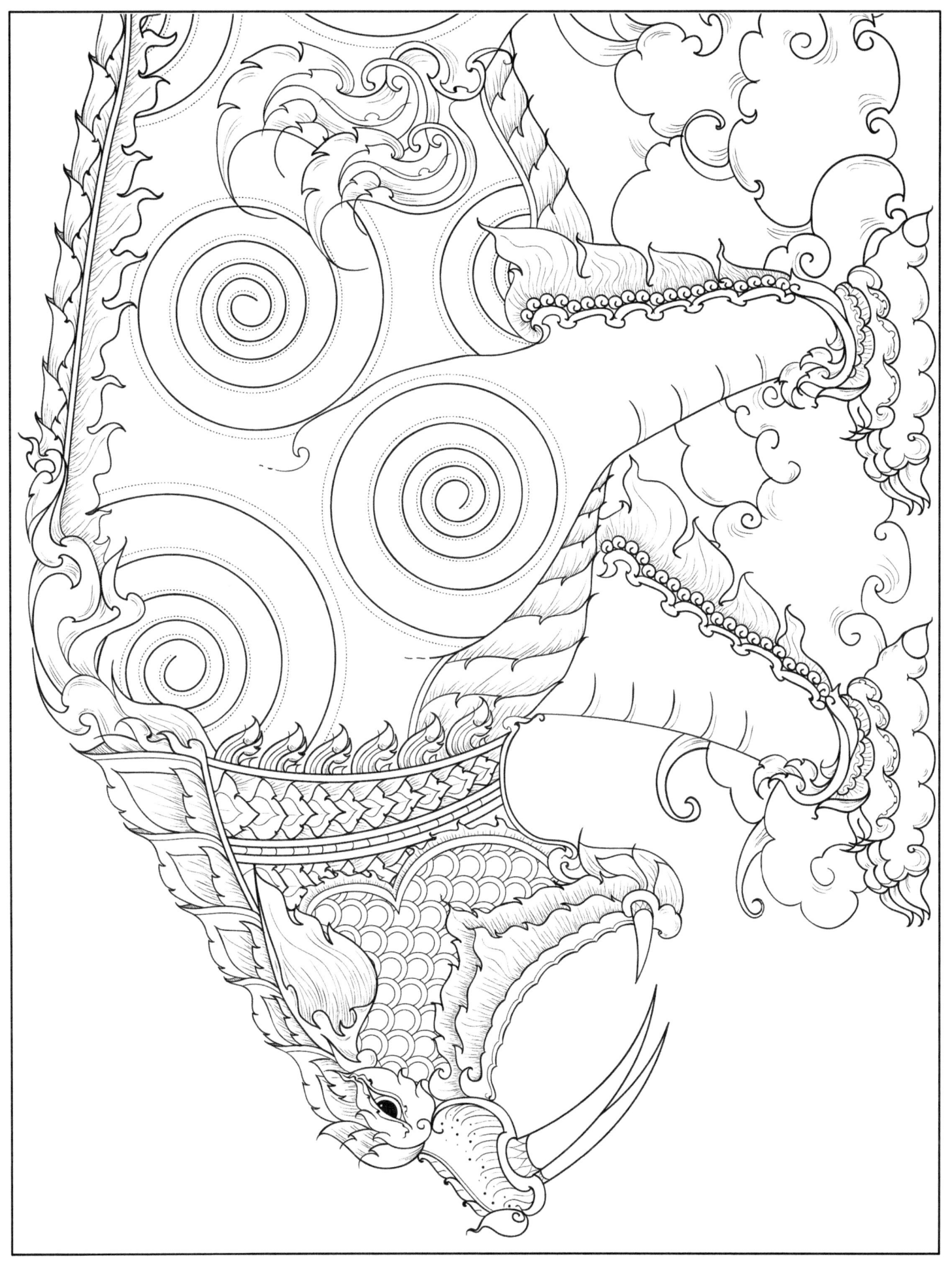

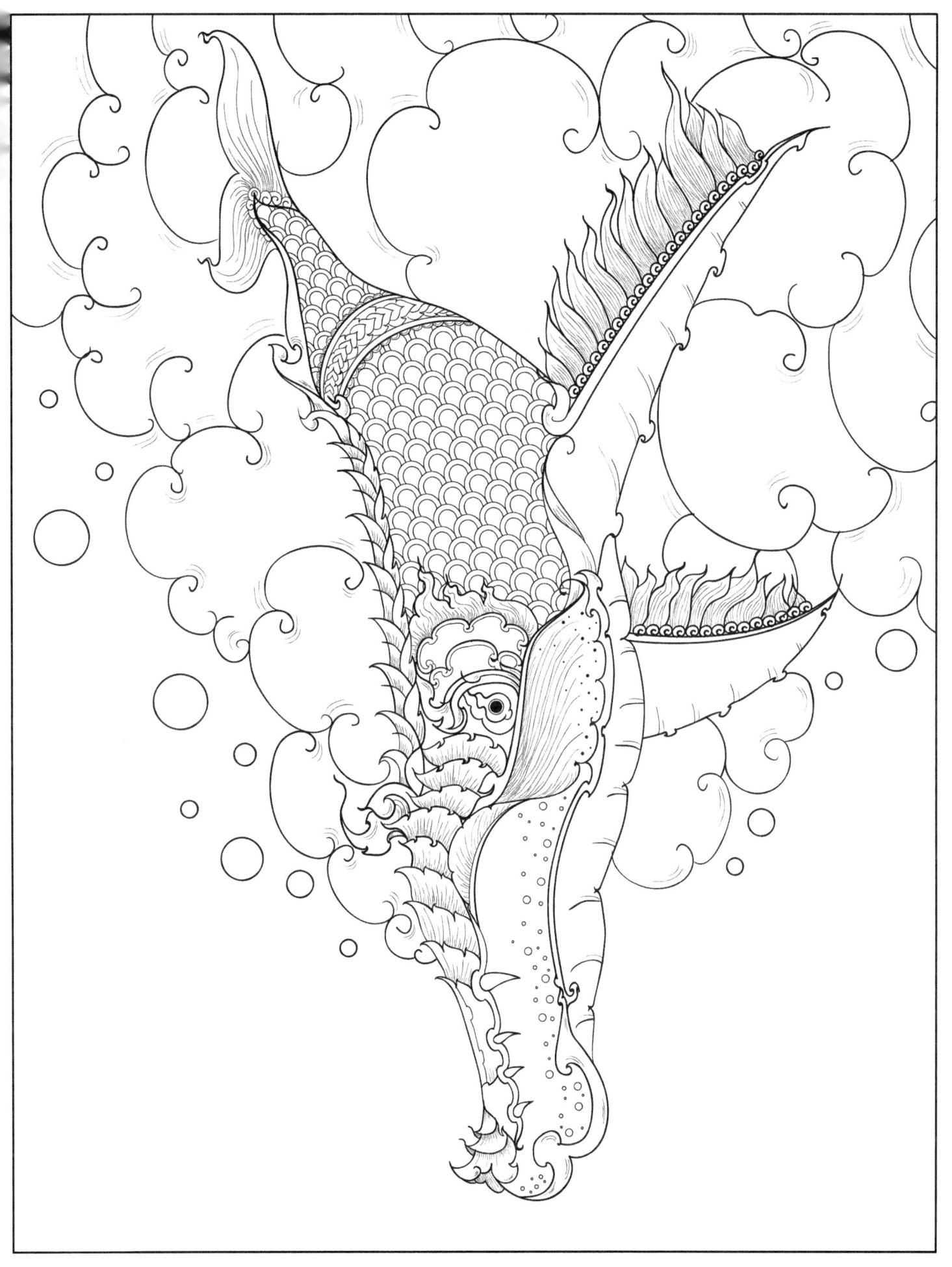

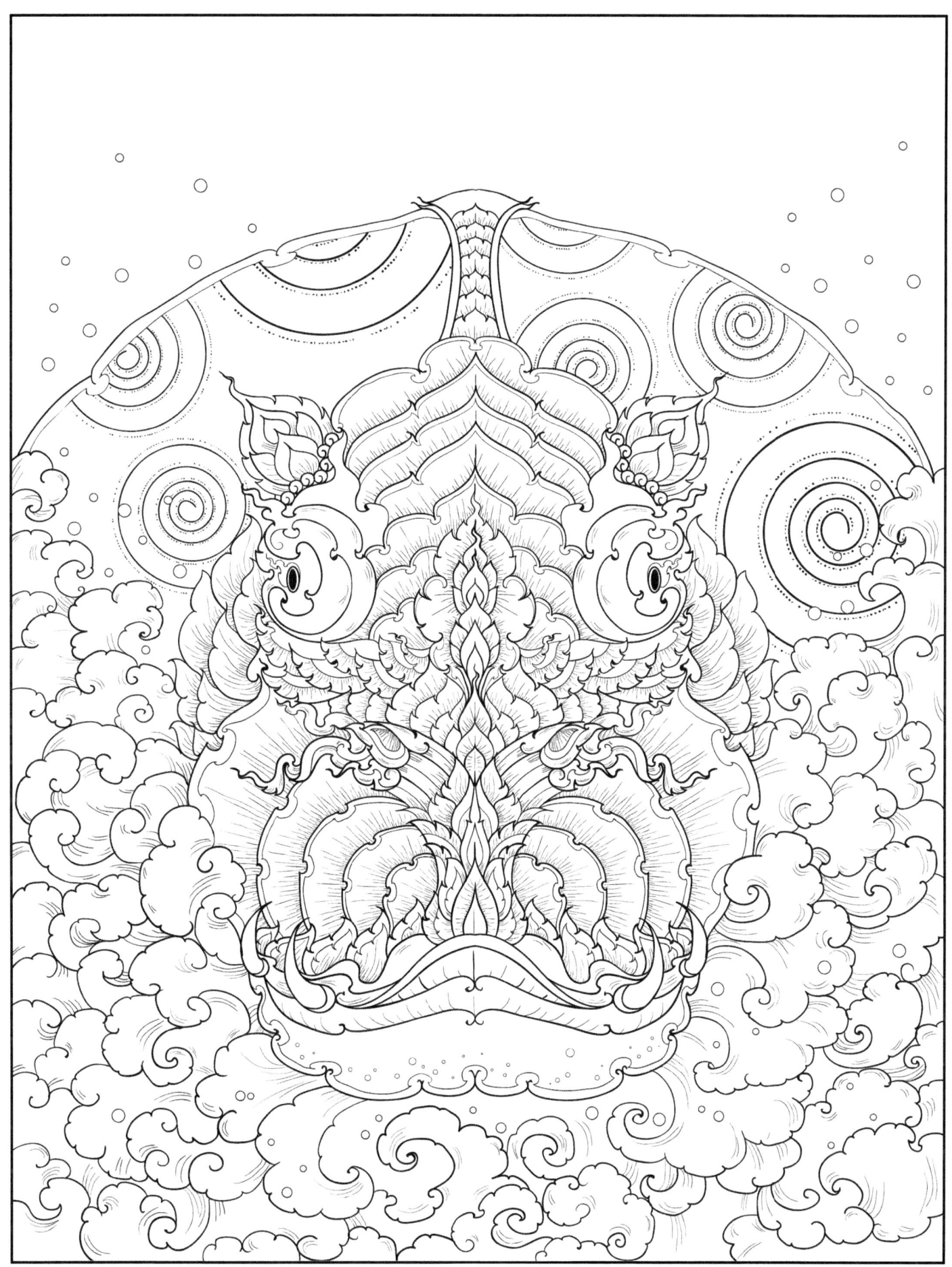

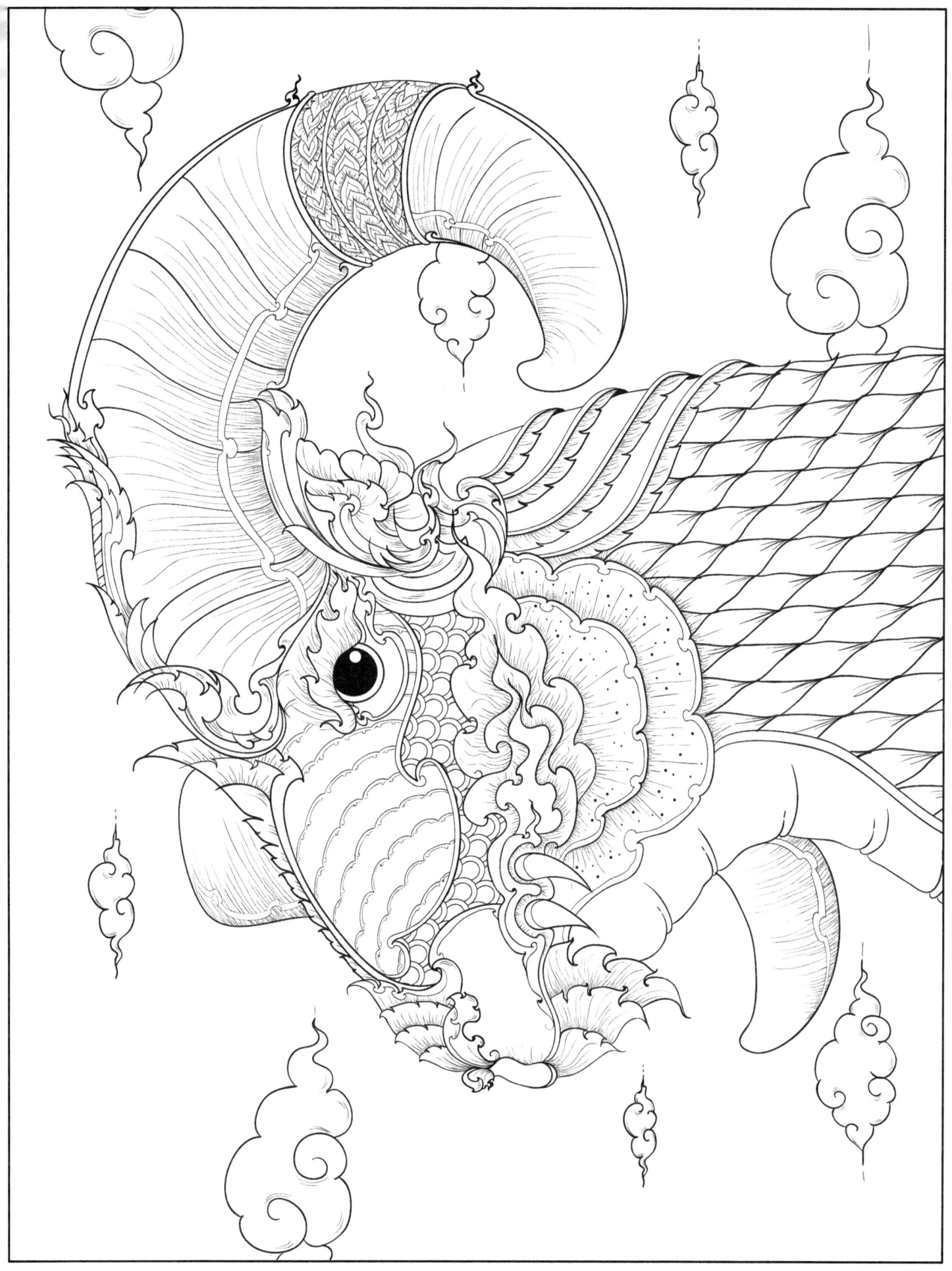

Exclusive Offer
ONLY V Art Studio Fan Club!!

Join V Art Group : *http://bit.ly/join_cover*

- Coloring Challenge : Selected Works will be published in Our New Release and you also will get the commission of Sales (First 3 Months)

- Participate in Creating Our New Book : Book Cover Vote , Coloring Idea and more.. / Your name will be appear in our book.

- GET Free Coloring Pages/ New Coloring Books for Our New Release.

- Much More ...

Join Us at : *http://bit.ly/join_cover*

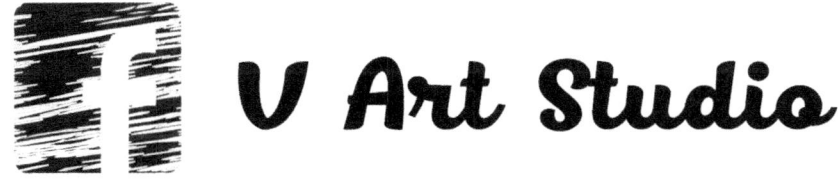